Table of Contents

Introduction 2

How to Use My Book 3

Great Granny Quilt 4

Great Granny Quilt Label 10

The Bonus Quilt 16

The Bonus Quilt Label 22

Great Granny Tablerunner . . . 26

Great Granny Pillow 30

Great Granny Squared

Introduction

The very first thing my Grandma Ewell taught me to crochet was granny squares. I fell in love with the scrappy look of granny squares way back then, using bits and pieces of leftover yarn. This very well could have started my romance with scrappy happy quilting.

These crocheted granny squares became the inspiration for the very first quilt along on my blog, Bee in my Bonnet. I was smitten by the cuteness of granny squares made from fabric as well as yarn, turning the traditional block known as the "Album Block" into a granny block! I designed a simplified way to construct the block as I considered how to use my fabric stash with these granny squares, specifically the precuts that were piling up in my studio.

My solution was to make my block bigger to use up more scraps, so I added an extra round of squares to the original granny square. My "Great Granny Block" was born!

Why the name, you ask?

The center square of the block is "The Baby". The four squares surrounding The Baby I appropriately named "The Mama". The eight squares surrounding The Mama are "The Granny", and of course the final twelve squares surrounding The Granny are (can you guess?) "The Great Granny"! Four generations of women all together in one block.

Another wonderful thing about my Great Granny Block is that it is friendly to all quilters. While it might look like a fussy block to piece, anyone can master my method of making this block!

So, I introduced my Great Granny Block on my blog, and I invited anyone and everyone to join me in making blocks for my very first quilt along, the Great Granny Along. Quilters flocked to the call, and I loved every single block and quilt I saw!

Now, I've taken my Great Granny Block to the next level. My original block uses 2 ½" squares, which can be cut from those wonderful 2 ½" strip rolls and many other fabric precuts (less waste, wouldn't Mom and Grandma be proud!). In this book, in addition to the original block, I've expanded it to use several different sizes of squares. Fear not, they still use precuts, so you can still be economical with your stash! *Waste not – want not!*

Above all, what a wonderful way to pay tribute to the generations of creative women that came before us! Our mothers, grandmothers, great-grandmothers and beyond … they continue to inspire us and shape our creative arts.

That makes me want to start digging through my scraps and start another Great Granny Block – so let's start sewing!

How to Use My Book

Before you delve into my book, here is what you need to know about my Great Granny Squared projects.

No Square Left Behind

Nothing makes me happier than patchwork full of bright, happy colors. To achieve a scrappy look, I used a total of 33 fat quarters in the Great Granny Quilt. Though it is possible to make my Great Granny Quilt with fewer fabrics, you would lose the charm of my scrappy happy look. After you have pieced the Great Granny Quilt, you will have 478 leftover squares. Before you wonder what to do with them, let me show you! I put all of these squares to good use in the Great Granny Quilt Label and The Bonus Quilt. For a scrappy look in my other projects, the Great Granny Tablerunner uses 1 ½" strips, and the Great Granny Pillow uses 3 ½" squares. Waste not, my friends!

Big Block, Little Block

From my Great Granny Block, you have many block size and style options. Each main project showcases a different block. The Great Granny Quilt shows the full block (with The Baby all the way to The Great Granny) finishing at 12". The Bonus Quilt is a variation of the block using only The Baby and The Mama squares and finishes at 6". The Great Granny Tablerunner miniaturizes the full block to a cute 6", and the Great Granny Pillow expands it to a whopping 20". Have fun and get creative with the possibilities!

Details, Details

For this book, I have included two quilt labels that can be embellished with embroidery, along with templates for the drawings and letters. I love to embroider my name, the date my quilt was made and any other details I want to remember. Labels are adorable and useful additions that will make your quilts all the sweeter.

Spice of Life

I encourage you to play with your color and fabric selections to your heart's desire on a design board. I have had great fun scrapping up my quilts and making each block in different color combinations. After all, variety is the spice of a quilty kind of life! ✽

Visit my blog for a tutorial on how to make my design board!

Great Granny Quilt

Finished Size: 72" x 85 ½"

Cutting Instructions:

From 33 fat quarters: (see cutting diagram)
- Cut 1   2 ½" square (33 total) *   Fabric A
- Cut 4   2 ½" squares (132 total) *   Fabric B
- Cut 8   2 ½" squares (264 total) *   Fabric C
- Cut 12   2 ½" squares (396 total) *   Fabric D
- Cut 5   2 ½" squares (165 total) *   Fabric E
- Cut 2   5" squares (66 total)   Fabric F
- Cut 1   2 ½" x 11" strip (33 total)   Fabric G

From 5 ⅝ yards of white background fabric:
- Cut 240   2 ½" x 3 ½" rectangles   Fabric H
- Cut 80   2 ½" x 5" rectangles   Fabric I
- Cut 31   2 ½" x 12 ½" strips   Fabric J
- Cut 248   2 ¾" squares   Fabric K
- Cut 4   2 ¾" x width of fabric strips   Fabric L
- Cut 12   2 ½" x width of fabric strips   Fabric M

From 5 ⅓ yards of backing fabric:
- Cut 2   41 ½" x 95 ½" rectangles   Fabric N

* To achieve my scrappy look, use 33 fat quarters. You will have 478 leftover 2 ½" squares. Save your leftover fabrics to use in the Great Granny Quilt Label on page 10 and The Bonus Quilt on page 16. If you are making only the Great Granny Quilt, it is still necessary to use the cutting instructions above since the block requires specific fabric placement.

Fat Quarter Cutting Diagram:

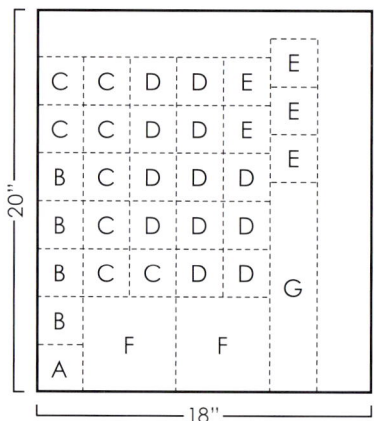

Great Granny Squared

Use ¼" seams and press as arrows indicate throughout.

Great Granny Blocks:

Before sewing each of the twenty Great Granny Blocks, lay out four different fabrics on your design board to visualize your block.

Each Great Granny Block has:
- one Baby square (Fabric A)
- four Mama squares (Fabric B)
- eight Granny squares (Fabric C)
- twelve Great Granny squares (Fabric D)

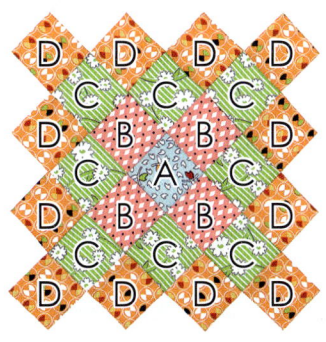

Assemble two Fabric H rectangles and one Fabric D square.

Strip One should measure 2 ½" x 8 ½".

Make two for each block. Make forty.

Make two for each block. Make forty.

Assemble two Fabric H rectangles, two matching Fabric D squares and one Fabric C square.

Strip Two should measure 2 ½" x 12 ½".

Make two for each block. Make forty.

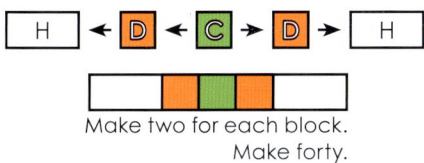

Make two for each block. Make forty.

Assemble two Fabric H rectangles, two matching Fabric D squares, two matching Fabric C squares and one Fabric B square.

Strip Three should measure 2 ½" x 16 ½".

Make two for each block. Make forty.

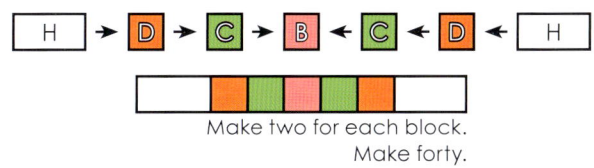

Make two for each block. Make forty.

Assemble two matching Fabric D squares, two matching Fabric C squares, two matching Fabric B squares and one Fabric A square.

Strip Four should measure 2 ½" x 14 ½".

Make one for each block. Make twenty.

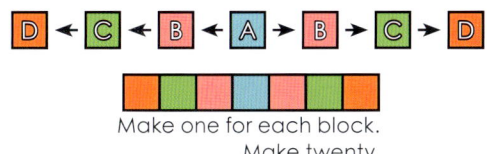

Make one for each block. Make twenty.

Assemble two matching Strip Ones, two matching Strip Twos, two matching Strip Threes and one Strip Four.

Match each seam intersection so seams nest.

Make twenty Great Granny Strip Units.

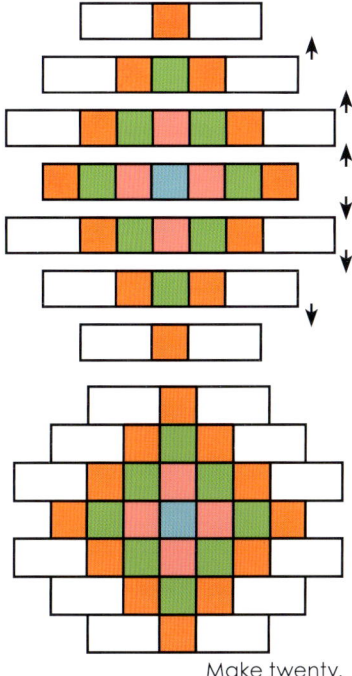

Make twenty.

Great Granny Squared

Great Granny Quilt

Trim the left and right sides off each Great Granny Strip Unit.

Make twenty.

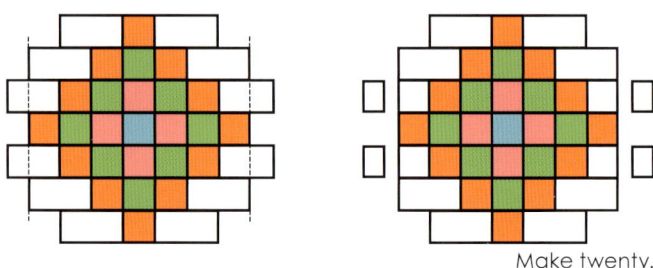

Make twenty.

Assemble four Fabric I rectangles to a Great Granny Strip Unit by matching centers for placement.

Make twenty Great Granny Block Units.

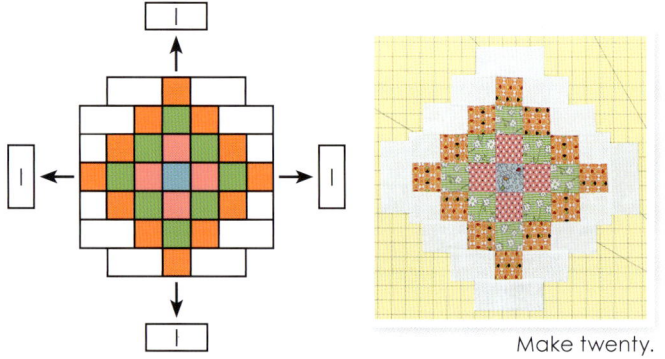

Make twenty.

Center a 12 ½" square ruler on a Great Granny Block Unit. I like to use the Creative Grids 12 ½" Square It Up Ruler.

Trim Great Granny Block to measure 12 ½" x 12 ½".

Make twenty.

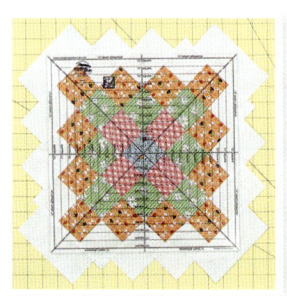
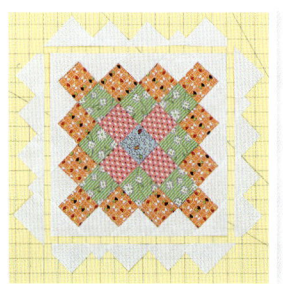

Make twenty.

Great Granny Rows:

Assemble four Great Granny Blocks and three Fabric J rectangles.

Great Granny Row should measure 12 ½" x 54 ½".

Make five.

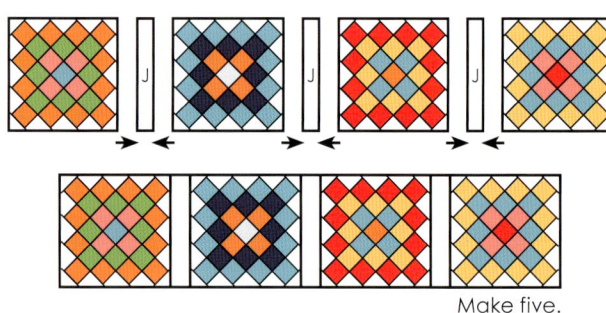

Make five.

Sashing Rows:

Assemble four Fabric J rectangles and three Fabric E squares.

Sashing Row should measure 2 ½" x 54 ½".

Make four.

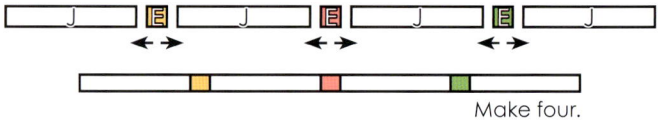

Make four.

Quilt Center:

Assemble five Great Granny Rows and four Sashing Rows.

Quilt Center should measure 54 ½" x 68 ½".

6 Great Granny Squared

Inner Borders:

Piece 2 ¾" Fabric L strips end to end.

Subcut into:

2 - 2 ¾" x 68 ½" strips (side inner borders)

Piece 2 ½" Fabric M strips end to end.

Subcut into:

2 - 2 ½" x 59" strips (top and bottom inner borders - M1)

2 - 2 ½" x 81 ½" strips (side outer borders - M2)

2 - 2 ½" x 72" strips (top and bottom outer borders - M3)

Attach side inner borders using the Fabric L strips.

Attach top and bottom inner borders using the Fabric M1 strips.

Middle Borders:

Draw a diagonal line on the wrong side of the Fabric K squares.

With right sides facing, layer two Fabric K squares on opposite corners of a Fabric F square.

Stitch on the drawn line and trim ¼" away from the seam.

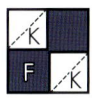 

Make sixty-two.

Repeat on the remaining two corners of the Fabric F square.

Diamond Unit should measure 5" x 5".

You will not use all Fabric F squares.

Make sixty-two.

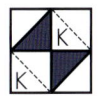 

Make sixty-two.

Great Granny Squared

Great Granny Quilt

Assemble sixteen Diamond Units.

Side Diamond Border Strip should measure 5" x 72 ½".

Make two.

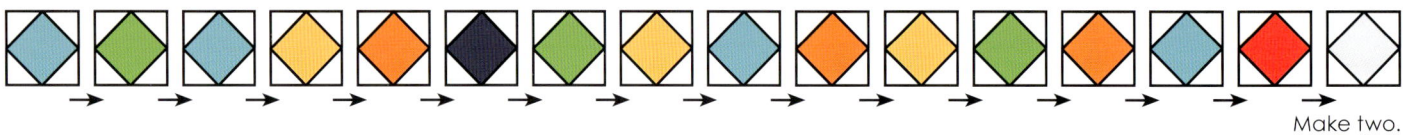

Make two.

Assemble fifteen Diamond Units.

Top and Bottom Diamond Border Strip should measure 5" x 68".

Make two.

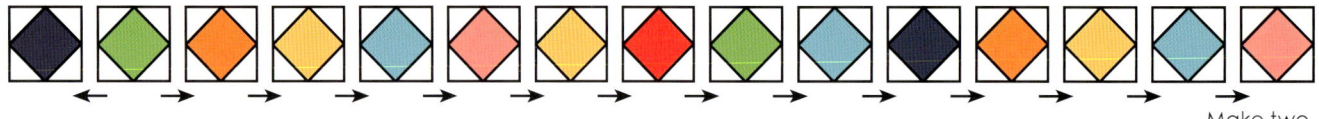

Make two.

Attach side middle borders using the Side Diamond Border Strips.

Attach top and bottom middle borders using the Top and Bottom Diamond Border Strips.

Outer Borders:

Attach side outer borders using the Fabric M2 strips.

Attach top and bottom outer borders using the Fabric M3 strips.

Scrappy Binding:

Piece Fabric G rectangles end to end to make the scrappy binding.

Press seams open for less bulk.

You need approximately 345" for binding.

Backing:

With right sides facing, piece the Fabric N rectangles together with a ½" seam.

Press open for less bulk.

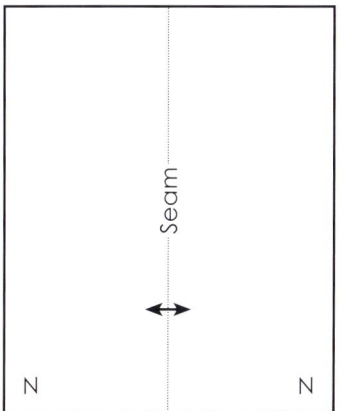

Finishing:

Quilt and bind as desired.

Great Granny Squared

Great Granny Quilt Label

Cutting Instructions:

From 1 ¼ yards of white background fabric:

- Cut 1	5" x 7 ½" rectangle	Fabric A
- Cut 2	3" squares	Fabric B
- Cut 2	2" squares	Fabric C
- Cut 2	1 ½" x 6" rectangles	Fabric D
- Cut 2	1 ½" x 3" rectangles	Fabric E
- Cut 4	1 ½" x 2 ½" rectangles	Fabric F
- Cut 2	1 ½" x 2" rectangles	Fabric G
- Cut 8	1 ½" squares	Fabric H
- Cut 1	1 ½" square	Fabric I
- Cut 2	2" x 15 ½" strips	Fabric J
- Cut 1	2 ½" x 14 ½" strip	Fabric K
- Cut 1	1 ½" x 14 ½" strip	Fabric L
- Cut 1	18 ½" x 22 ½" rectangle	Fabric M

From a fat quarter of pink fabric for basket base:

- Cut 1	5 ½" x 11 ½" rectangle	Fabric N
- Cut 1	2" x 9 ½" rectangle	Fabric O

From ⅛ yard of red fabric for basket handle and trim:

- Cut 1	1 ½" x 6 ½" rectangle	Fabric P
- Cut 2	1 ½" x 6" rectangles	Fabric Q
- Cut 4	1 ½" squares	Fabric R
- Cut 1	1 ½" square	Fabric S

From ⅛ yard of blue fabric for basket bow:

- Cut 2	1 ½" x 3 ½" rectangles	Fabric T
- Cut 6	1 ½" x 2 ½" rectangles	Fabric U
- Cut 1	1 ½" square	Fabric V

From leftover 2 ½" squares from the Great Granny Quilt:

- 36	2 ½" squares *	Fabric W

Embroidery floss

Finished Size: 18" x 22"

* If you are not using leftover fabrics from the Great Granny Quilt, cut squares from your scrappy stash.

Use ¼" seams and press as arrows indicate throughout.

Basket Block:

Draw a diagonal line on the wrong side of the Fabric H squares.

With right sides facing, layer a Fabric H square on one end of a Fabric U rectangle.

Stitch on the drawn line and trim ¼" away from the seam.

Fabric U/H Unit should measure 1 ½" x 2 ½".

Make four.

Make two
Left Fabric U/H Units.

Make two
Right Fabric U/H Units.

Draw a diagonal line on the wrong side of the Fabric R squares.

With right sides facing, layer a Fabric R square on one end of a Fabric U rectangle.

Stitch on the drawn line and trim ¼" away from the seam.

Fabric U/R Unit should measure 1 ½" x 2 ½".

Make two.

Make one
Left Fabric U/R Unit.

Make one
Right Fabric U/R Unit.

Assemble one Fabric U/H Unit, one Fabric F rectangle and one Fabric U/R Unit.

Bow Middle Unit should measure 2 ½" x 3 ½".

Make two.

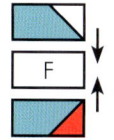  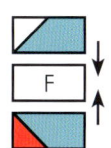 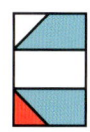

Make one
Left Bow Middle Unit.

Make one
Right Bow Middle Unit.

With right sides facing, layer a Fabric R square on one end of a Fabric T rectangle.

Stitch on the drawn line and trim ¼" away from the seam.

Make one
Left Bow End Unit.

Make one
Right Bow End Unit.

Repeat on the opposite end of the Fabric T rectangle with a Fabric H square.

Bow End Unit should measure 1 ½" x 3 ½".

Make two.

Make one
Left Bow End Unit.

Make one
Right Bow End Unit.

Assemble the Fabric I square, the Fabric V square and the Fabric S square.

Bow Center Unit should measure 1 ½" x 3 ½".

Make one.

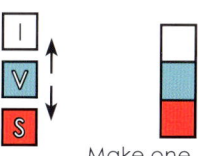

Make one.

Assemble the Left Bow End Unit, the Left Bow Middle Unit, the Bow Center Unit, the Right Bow Middle Unit and the Right Bow End Unit.

Top Bow Unit should measure 3 ½" x 7 ½".

Make one.

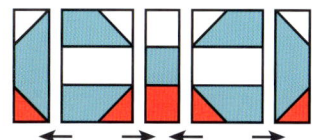 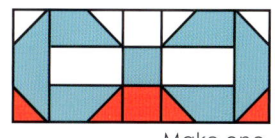

Make one.

Assemble one Fabric F rectangle and one Fabric U/H Unit.

Fabric F/U/H Unit should measure 2 ½" x 2 ½".

Make two.

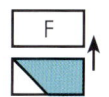

Make one
Left Fabric F/U/H Unit.

Make one
Right Fabric F/U/H Unit.

Great Granny Quilt Label

With right sides facing, layer a Fabric H square on one end of a Fabric Q rectangle.

Stitch on the drawn line and trim ¼" away from the seam.

Fabric H/Q Unit should measure 1 ½" x 6".

Make two.

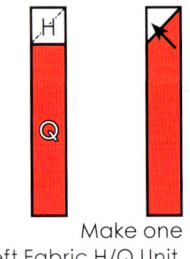
Make one
Left Fabric H/Q Unit.

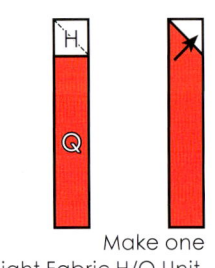
Make one
Right Fabric H/Q Unit.

Assemble one Fabric D rectangle and one Fabric H/Q Unit.

Handle Unit should measure 2 ½" x 6".

Make two.

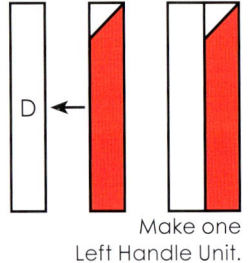
Make one
Left Handle Unit.

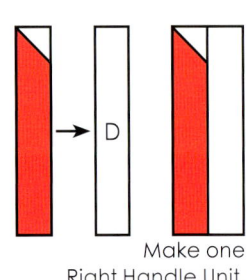
Make one
Right Handle Unit.

Assemble one Fabric F/U/H Unit and one Handle Unit.

Handle/Bow Unit should measure 2 ½" x 8".

Make two.

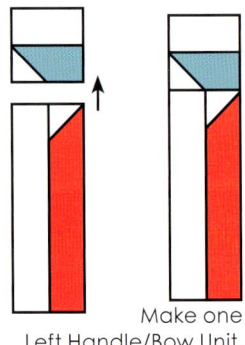
Make one
Left Handle/Bow Unit.

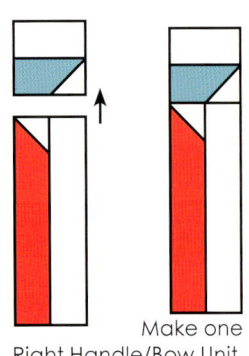
Make one
Right Handle/Bow Unit.

Assemble the Top Bow Unit and the Fabric A rectangle.

Bow Unit should measure 7 ½" x 8".

Make one.

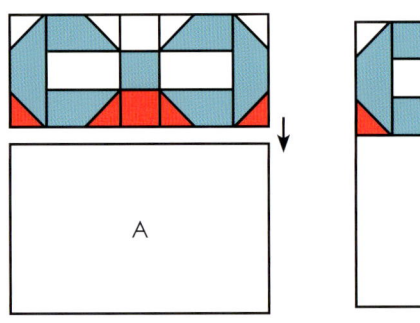
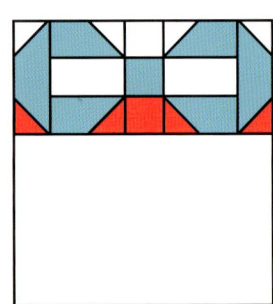
Make one.

Assemble the Left Handle/Bow Unit, the Bow Unit and the Right Handle/Bow Unit.

Top Basket Unit should measure 8" x 11 ½".

Make one.

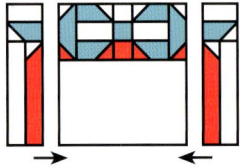

Make one.

Draw a diagonal line on the wrong side of the Fabric B squares.

With right sides facing, layer a Fabric B square on the bottom left corner of the Fabric N rectangle.

Stitch on the drawn line and trim ¼" away from the seam.

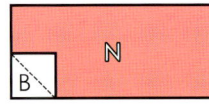
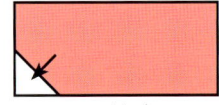
Make one.

Repeat on the bottom right corner of the Fabric N rectangle.

Middle Basket Unit should measure 5 ½" x 11 ½".

Make one.

Make one.

12 Great Granny Squared

Assemble two Fabric E rectangles and the Fabric P rectangle.

Trim Unit should measure 1 ½" x 11 ½".

Make one.

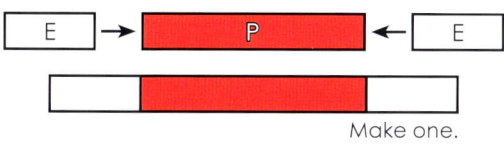

Make one.

Draw a diagonal line on the wrong side of the Fabric C squares.

With right sides facing, layer a Fabric C square on the left end of the Fabric O rectangle.

Stitch on the drawn line and trim ¼" away from the seam.

Make one.

Repeat on the right end of the Fabric O rectangle.

Fabric C/O/C Unit should measure 2" x 9 ½".

Make one.

Make one.

Assemble two Fabric G rectangles and the Fabric C/O/C Unit.

Bottom Basket Unit should measure 2" x 11 ½".

Make one.

Make one.

Assemble the Top Basket Unit, the Middle Basket Unit, the Trim Unit and the Bottom Basket Unit.

Basket Block should measure 11 ½" x 15 ½".

Make one.

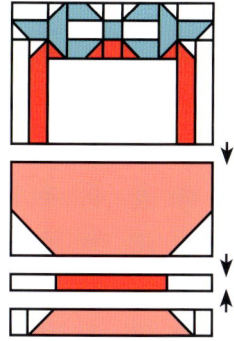 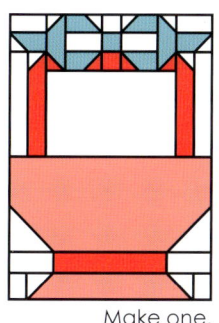

Make one.

Inner Borders:

Attach side inner borders using the Fabric J strips.

Attach top inner border using the Fabric L strip.

Attach bottom inner border using the Fabric K strip.

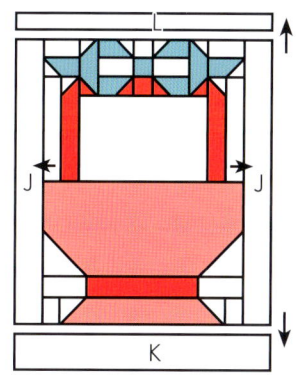

Outer Borders:

Assemble nine Fabric W squares.

Patchwork Outer Border should measure 2 ½" x 18 ½".

Make four.

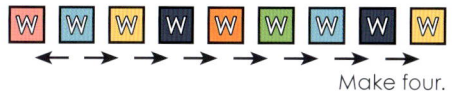

Make four.

Attach side outer borders using two Patchwork Outer Borders.

Attach top and bottom outer borders using two Patchwork Outer Borders.

Great Granny Quilt Label should measure 18 ½" x 22 ½".

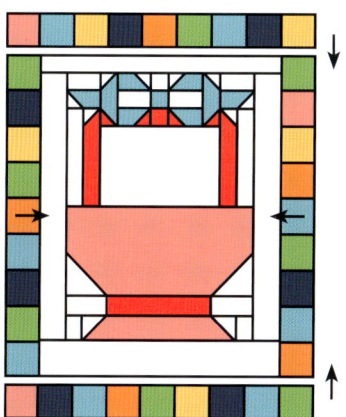

Great Granny Quilt Label

Embroidery:

Using the template below, trace the embroidery pattern above the basket base.

Using three strands of embroidery floss, sew a backstitch for the lines and a French knot with three twists for the dots.

Use the template below to add the finishing touches to your label. Trace the embroidery pattern below the basket.

2014 by Lori Holt of Bee in my Bonnet :)

0123456789

ABCDEFGHIJKLMNOPQRSTUVWXYZ

abcdefghijklmnopqrstuvwxyz

Label Backing:

With right sides facing, layer the Great Granny Quilt Label with the Fabric M rectangle.

Stitch around the Great Granny Quilt Label using a ¼" seam. Leave an 8" opening at the bottom.

Turn the Great Granny Quilt Label right side out.

Press the opening edges under ¼" and hand stitch the bottom closed.

Great Granny Quilt Label should measure 18" x 22".

8" Opening

Attaching the Label:

Pin the Great Granny Quilt Label 10" to 12" from the side and bottom of the Great Granny Quilt backing, leaving plenty of room for the longarm quilter to put it on their longarm frame without bothering the label.

Use a whip stitch to sew the Great Granny Quilt Label to the backing.

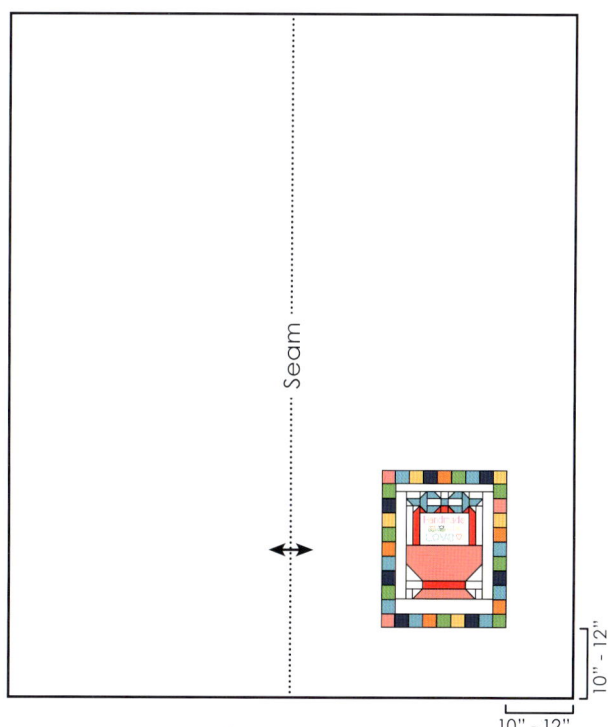

The Bonus Quilt

Finished Size: 54 ½" x 66 ½"

Cutting Instructions:

From leftover 2 ½ squares from the Great Granny Quilt and the Great Granny Quilt Label:

- 28   2 ½" squares *   Fabric A
- 112   2 ½" squares *   Fabric B
- 167   2 ½" squares *   Fabric C

From 4 yards of navy background fabric:

- Cut 112   2 ½" squares   Fabric D
- Cut 112   2 ½" x 3 ½" rectangles   Fabric E
- Cut 32   1 ½" x 6 ½" rectangles   Fabric F
- Cut 11   1 ½" x width of fabric strips   Fabric G
- Cut 7   6 ½" x width of fabric strips   Fabric H
- Cut 7   2 ½" x width of fabric strips   Fabric I

From 4 ¼ yards of backing fabric:

- Cut 2   32 ¾" x 76 ½" rectangles   Fabric J

* If you are not using leftover fabrics from the Great Granny Quilt or the Great Granny Quilt Label, cut eleven 2 ½" squares from 33 different fabrics. You will have leftover fabrics since the block requires specific fabric placement.

16   Great Granny Squared

Use ¼" seams and press as arrows indicate throughout.

Mama Blocks:

Before sewing each of the twenty-eight Mama Blocks, lay out two different fabrics on your design board to visualize your block.

Each Mama Block has:
- one Baby square (Fabric A)
- four Mama squares (Fabric B)

Assemble two Fabric D squares and one Fabric B square.

Strip One should measure 2 ½" x 6 ½".

Make two for each block. Make fifty-six.

Make two for each block. Make fifty-six.

Assemble two matching Fabric B squares and one Fabric A square.

Strip Two should measure 2 ½" x 6 ½".

Make one for each block. Make twenty-eight.

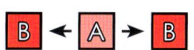   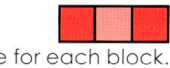

Make one for each block. Make twenty-eight.

Assemble two matching Strip Ones and one Strip Two.

Mama Strip Unit should measure 6 ½" x 6 ½".

Make twenty-eight.

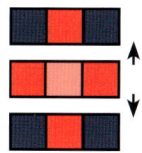   

Make twenty-eight.

Assemble four Fabric E rectangles to a Mama Strip Unit by matching centers for placement.

Make twenty-eight Mama Block Units.

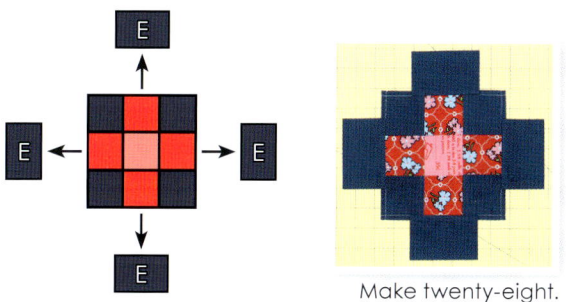

Make twenty-eight.

Center a 6 ½" square ruler on a Mama Block Unit. I like to use the Creative Grids 6 ½" Square It Up Ruler.

Trim Mama Block to measure 6 ½" x 6 ½".

Make twenty-eight.

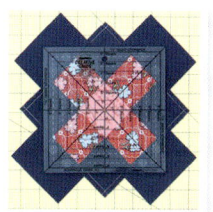   

Make twenty-eight.

Great Granny Squared   17

The Bonus Quilt

Mama Rows:

Assemble eight Fabric F rectangles and seven Mama Blocks.

Mama Row should measure 6 ½" x 50 ½".

Make four.

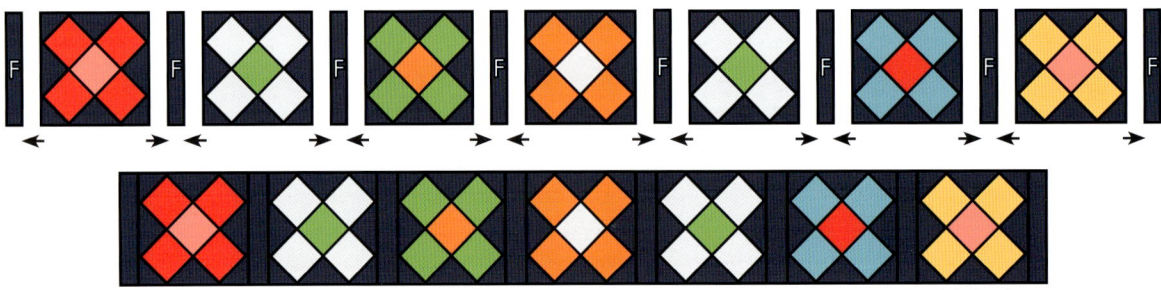

Make four.

Patchwork Sashing Rows:

Assemble twenty-five Fabric C squares.

Side Patchwork Sashing Row should measure 2 ½" x 50 ½".

Make five.

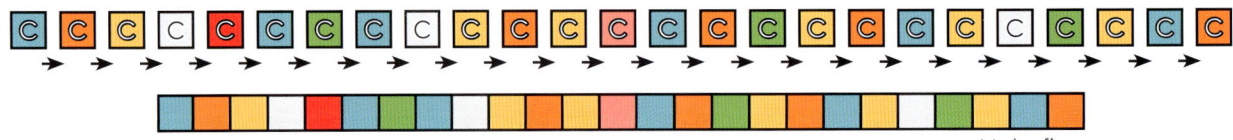

Make five.

Assemble twenty-one Fabric C squares.

Top and Bottom Patchwork Sashing Row should measure 2 ½" x 42 ½".

Make two.

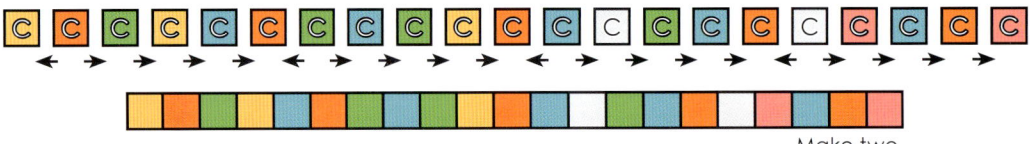

Make two.

18   Great Granny Squared

Quilt Center:

Piece 1 ½" Fabric G strips end to end.

Subcut into:

    8 - 1 ½" x 50 ½" strips (sashing rows)

Assemble five Side Patchwork Sashing Rows, eight Fabric G Sashing Rows and four Mama Rows.

Quilt Center Unit should measure 42 ½" x 50 ½".

Assemble Quilt Center Unit and two Top and Bottom Patchwork Sashing Rows.

Quilt Center should measure 42 ½" x 54 ½".

Great Granny Squared   19

The Bonus Quilt

Borders:

Piece 6 ½" Fabric H strips end to end.

Subcut into:

    4 - 6 ½" x 54 ½" (borders)

Attach side borders using two Fabric H strips.

Attach top and bottom borders using two Fabric H strips.

Binding:

Piece Fabric I strips end to end for binding.

Backing:

With right sides facing, piece the Fabric J rectangles together with a ½" seam.

Press open for less bulk.

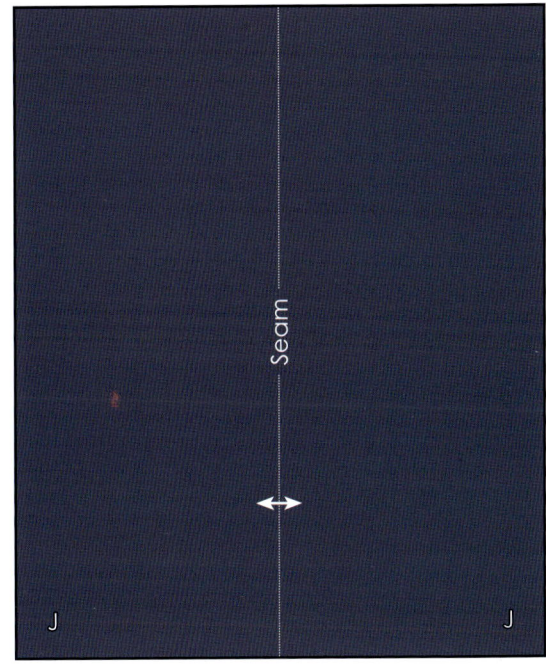

Finishing:

Quilt and bind as desired.

Great Granny Squared 21

The Bonus Quilt Label

Finished Size: 12" x 16"

Cutting Instructions:

From ¾ yard of navy background fabric:
- Cut 1   2" x 10 ½" rectangle — Fabric A
- Cut 2   1 ½" x 2" rectangles — Fabric B
- Cut 12   1 ½" squares — Fabric C
- Cut 1   1" x 10 ½" rectangle — Fabric D
- Cut 1   1" x 6 ¼" rectangle — Fabric E
- Cut 2   1" x 3 ½" rectangles — Fabric F
- Cut 2   1" squares — Fabric G
- Cut 2   1 ½" x 6 ½" rectangles — Fabric H
- Cut 2   1 ½" x 12 ½" rectangles — Fabric I
- Cut 1   12 ½" x 16 ½" rectangle — Fabric J

From a fat eighth of blue fabric for crochet hook:
- Cut 1   1" x 7 ½" rectangle — Fabric K
- Cut 1   1" x 1 ¾" rectangle — Fabric L

From 3 scrappy fabrics for yarn balls:
- Cut 1   3 ½" square (3 total) — Fabric M

From 4 scrappy fabrics for outer border:
- Cut 1   2 ½" x 12 ½" strip (4 total) — Fabric N

Embroidery floss

22   Great Granny Squared

Use ¼" seams and press as arrows indicate throughout.

Yarn and Crochet Hook Block:

Draw a diagonal line on the wrong side of the Fabric C squares.

With right sides facing, layer a Fabric C square on one corner of a Fabric M square.

Stitch on the drawn line and trim ¼" away from the seam.

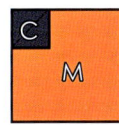 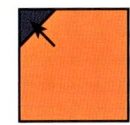

Make three.

Repeat on the remaining corners of the Fabric M square.

Yarn Unit should measure 3 ½" x 3 ½".

Make three.

 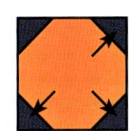

Make three.

Assemble three Yarn Units and two Fabric F rectangles.

Three Yarn Unit should measure 3 ½" x 10 ½".

Make one.

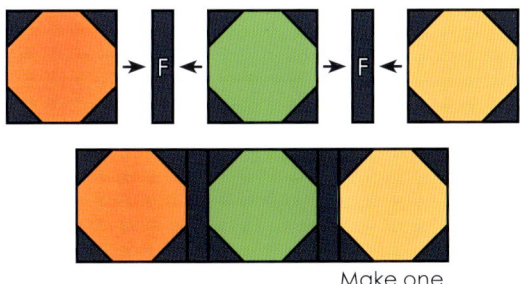

Make one.

Draw a diagonal line on the wrong side of the Fabric G squares.

With right sides facing, layer a Fabric G square on the left end of the Fabric L rectangle.

Stitch on the drawn line and trim ¼" away from the seam.

Make one.

Repeat on the right end of the Fabric L rectangle.

Fabric G/L/G Unit should measure 1" x 1 ¾".

Make one.

Make one.

Assemble the Fabric G/L/G Unit and the Fabric E rectangle.

Top Crochet Hook Unit should measure 1" x 7 ½".

Make one.

Make one.

Assemble the Top Crochet Hook Unit and the Fabric K rectangle.

Crochet Hook Unit should measure 1 ½" x 7 ½".

Make one.

Make one.

Assemble two Fabric B rectangles and the Crochet Hook Unit.

Crochet Hook Block should measure 1 ½" x 10 ½".

Make one.

Make one.

Great Granny Squared   23

The Bonus Quilt Label

Assemble the Fabric A rectangle, the Crochet Hook Block, the Fabric D rectangle and the Three Yarn Unit.

Yarn and Crochet Hook Block should measure 6 ½" x 10 ½".

Make one.

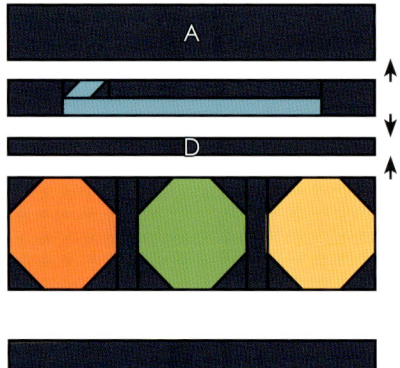

Make one.

Inner Borders:

Attach side inner borders using the Fabric H strips.

Attach top and bottom inner borders using the Fabric I strips.

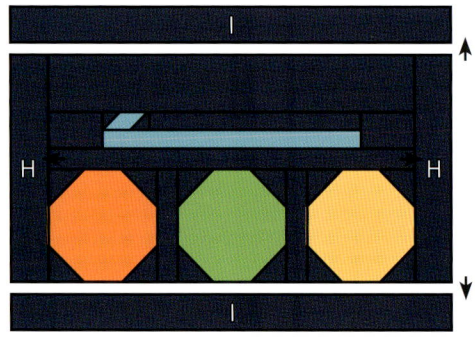

Outer Borders:

Attach top and bottom outer borders using two Fabric N strips.

Attach side outer borders using two Fabric N strips.

The Bonus Quilt Label should measure 12 ½" x 16 ½".

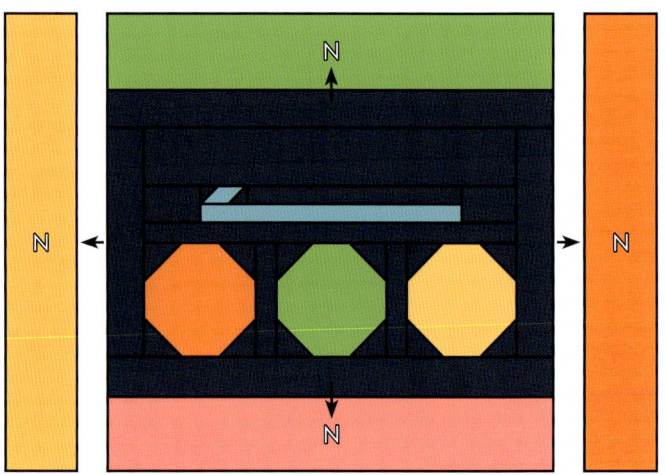

Embroidery:

Use the template to the left, along with your signature, to add the finishing touches to your label. Trace the embroidery pattern above the crochet hook.

Using three strands of embroidery floss, sew a backstitch for the lines and a French knot with three twists for the dots.

0123456789

Label Backing:

With right sides facing, layer The Bonus Quilt Label with the Fabric J rectangle.

Stitch around The Bonus Quilt Label using a ¼" seam. Leave an 8" opening at the bottom.

Turn The Bonus Quilt Label right side out.

Press the opening edges under ¼" and hand stitch the bottom closed.

The Bonus Quilt Label should measure 12" x 16".

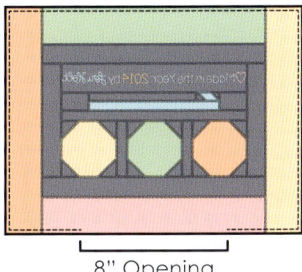
8" Opening

Attaching the Label:

Pin The Bonus Quilt Label 10" to 12" from the side and bottom of The Bonus Quilt backing, leaving plenty of room for the longarm quilter to put it on their longarm frame without bothering the label.

Use a whip stitch to sew The Bonus Quilt Label to the backing.

Great Granny Squared

Great Granny Tablerunner

Finished Size: 24 ½" x 45 ½"

Cutting Instructions:

From 21 1 ½" x width of fabric strips:
- Cut 1   1 ½" square (21 total) *   Fabric A
- Cut 4   1 ½" squares (84 total) *   Fabric B
- Cut 8   1 ½" squares (168 total) *   Fabric C
- Cut 12   1 ½" squares (252 total) *   Fabric D

From 1 ¾ yards of green background fabric:
- Cut 216 1 ½" x 2 ½" rectangles   Fabric E
- Cut 72   1 ½" x 3 ½" rectangles   Fabric F
- Cut 12   1 ½" x 6 ½" rectangles   Fabric G
- Cut 5   1 ½" x 20 ½" strips   Fabric H
- Cut 2   2 ½" x 41 ½" strips   Fabric I
- Cut 2   2 ½" x 24 ½" strips   Fabric J

From 1 ⅝ yards of binding and backing fabric:
(see cutting diagram)
- Cut 3   2 ½" x 58 ½" length of fabric strips   Fabric K
- Cut 1   32 ½" x 55 ½" rectangle   Fabric L

* Though the tablerunner can be made with 18 fabrics, I used 21 fabrics to achieve my scrappy happy look.

Binding and Backing Cutting Diagram:

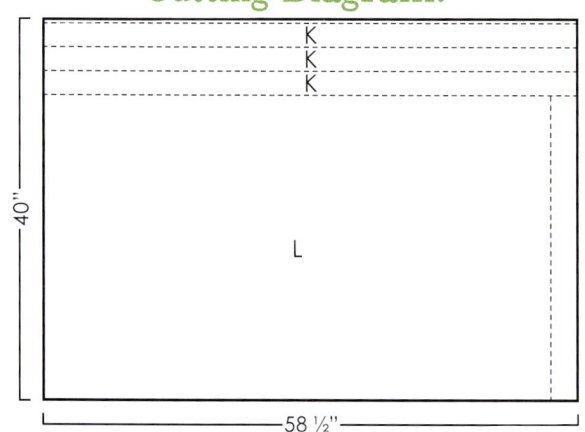

26   Great Granny Squared

Use ¼" seams and press as arrows indicate throughout.

Great Granny Blocks:

Before sewing each of the eighteen Great Granny Blocks, lay out four different fabrics on your design board to visualize your block.

Each Great Granny Block has:
- one Baby square (Fabric A)
- four Mama squares (Fabric B)
- eight Granny squares (Fabric C)
- twelve Great Granny squares (Fabric D)

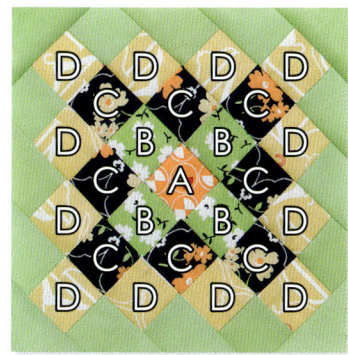

Assemble two Fabric E rectangles and one Fabric D square.

Strip One should measure 1 ½" x 5 ½".

Make two for each block. Make thirty-six.

Make two for each block.
Make thirty-six.

Assemble two Fabric E rectangles, two matching Fabric D squares and one Fabric C square.

Strip Two should measure 1 ½" x 7 ½".

Make two for each block. Make thirty-six.

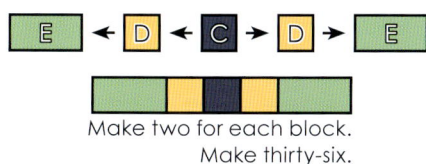

Make two for each block.
Make thirty-six.

Assemble two Fabric E rectangles, two matching Fabric D squares, two matching Fabric C squares and one Fabric B square.

Strip Three should measure 1 ½" x 9 ½".

Make two for each block. Make thirty-six.

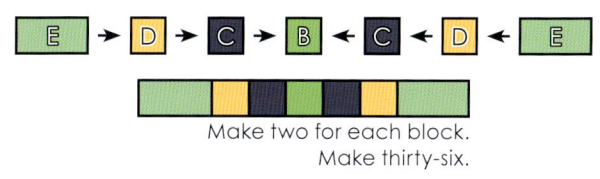

Make two for each block.
Make thirty-six.

Assemble two matching Fabric D squares, two matching Fabric C squares, two matching Fabric B squares and one Fabric A square.

Strip Four should measure 1 ½" x 7 ½".

You will not use all Fabric A, Fabric B, Fabric C and Fabric D squares.

Make one for each block. Make eighteen.

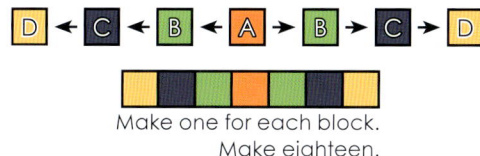

Make one for each block.
Make eighteen.

Assemble two matching Strip Ones, two matching Strip Twos, two matching Strip Threes and one Strip Four.

Match each seam intersection so seams nest.

Make eighteen Great Granny Strip Units.

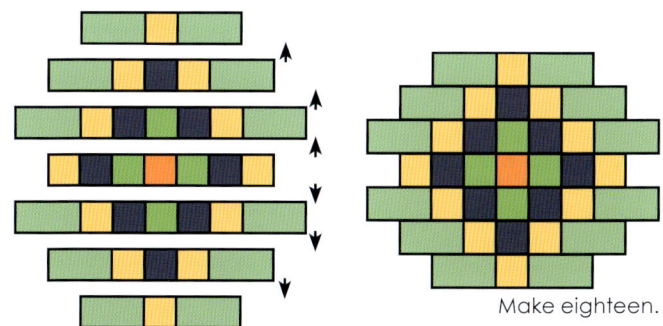

Make eighteen.

Great Granny Squared 27

Great Granny Tablerunner

Trim the left and right sides off each Great Granny Strip Unit.

Make eighteen.

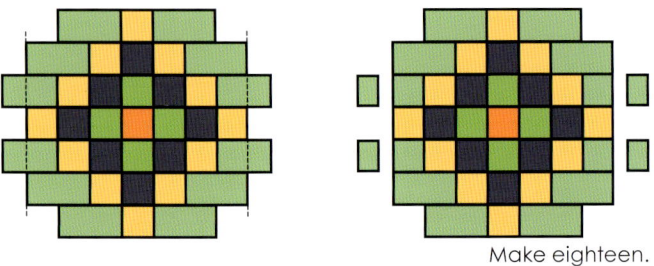

Make eighteen.

Assemble four Fabric F rectangles to a Great Granny Strip Unit by matching centers for placement.

Make eighteen Great Granny Block Units.

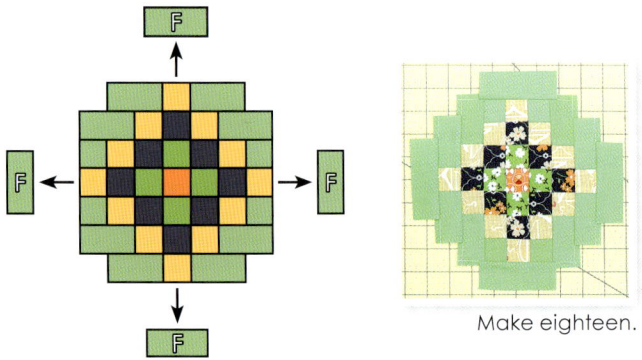

Make eighteen.

Center a 6 ½" square ruler on a Great Granny Block Unit. I like to use the Creative Grids 6 ½" Square It Up Ruler.

Trim Great Granny Block to measure 6 ½" x 6 ½".

Make eighteen.

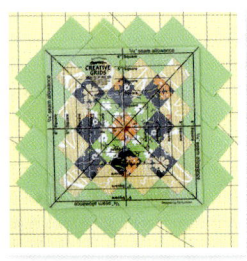

Make eighteen.

Great Granny Rows:

Assemble three Great Granny Blocks and two Fabric G rectangles.

Great Granny Row should measure 6 ½" x 20 ½".

Make six.

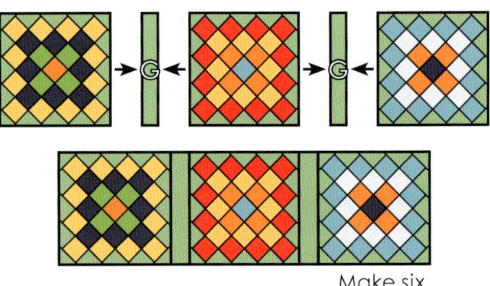

Make six.

Tablerunner Center:

Assemble six Great Granny Rows and five Fabric H strips.

Tablerunner Center should measure 20 ½" x 41 ½".

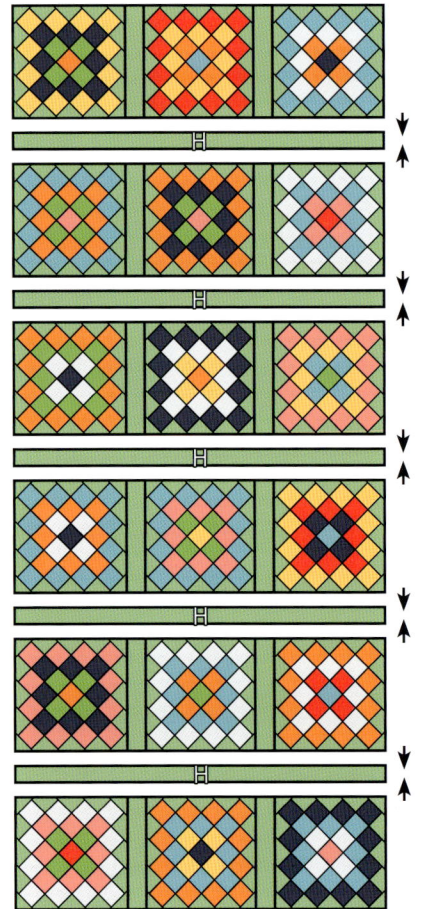

Borders:

Attach side borders using the Fabric I strips.

Attach top and bottom borders using the Fabric J strips.

Binding:

Piece Fabric K strips end to end for binding.

Backing:

Use the Fabric L rectangle for backing.

Finishing:

Quilt and bind as desired.

Great Granny Squared

Great Granny Pillow

Finished Size: 24 ½" x 24 ½"

Cutting Instructions:

From 24 scrappy fabrics:
- Cut 1   3 ½" square (24 total)   Fabric A

From ⅞ yard of pink background fabric:
- Cut 1   3 ½" square   Fabric B
- Cut 12   3 ½" x 6 ½" rectangles   Fabric C
- Cut 4   5" x 9 ½" rectangles   Fabric D
- Cut 2   2 ½" x 20 ½" strips   Fabric E
- Cut 2   2 ½" x 24 ½" strips   Fabric F

From 2 yards of backing and binding fabric:
- Cut 2   28" x 32" rectangles   Fabric G
- Cut 4   2 ½" x width of fabric strips   Fabric H

From muslin:
- Cut 1   28" square   Fabric I

From craft size package of batting:
- Cut 1   28" square   Batting

One 24" pillow form or a 26" pillow form for a fuller look

30   Great Granny Squared

Use ¼" seams and press as arrows indicate throughout.

Great Granny Block:

Assemble two Fabric C rectangles and one Fabric A square.

Strip One should measure 3 ½" x 15 ½".

Make two.

Make two.

Assemble two Fabric C rectangles and three Fabric A squares.

Strip Two should measure 3 ½" x 21 ½".

Make two.

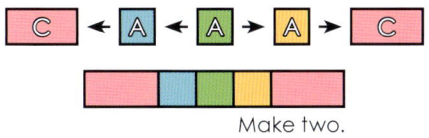

Make two.

Assemble two Fabric C rectangles and five Fabric A squares.

Strip Three should measure 3 ½" x 27 ½".

Make two.

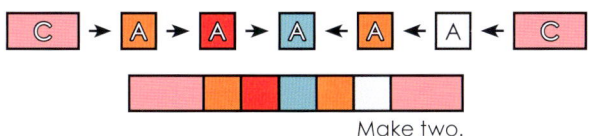

Make two.

Assemble six Fabric A squares and the Fabric B square.

Strip Four should measure 3 ½" x 21 ½".

Make one.

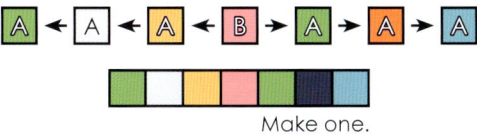

Make one.

Assemble two Strip Ones, two Strip Twos, two Strip Threes and one Strip Four.

Match each seam intersection so seams nest.

Make one Great Granny Strip Unit.

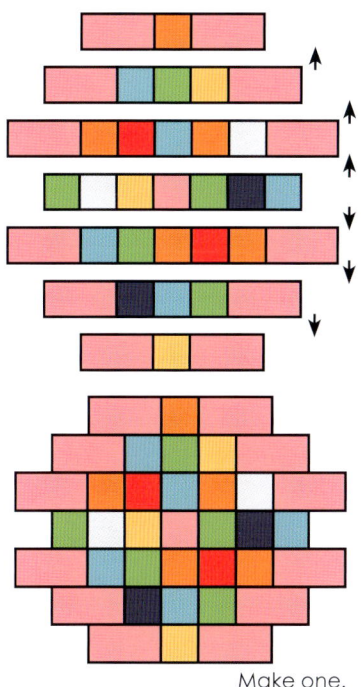

Make one.

Trim the left and right sides off the Great Granny Strip Unit.

Make one.

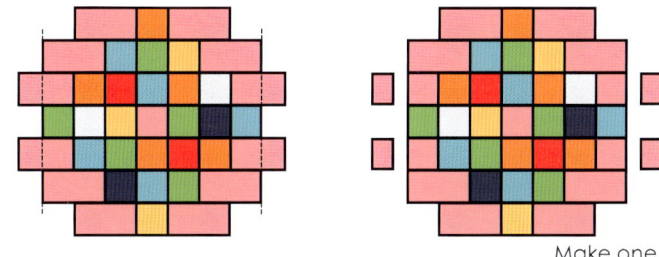

Make one.

Great Granny Squared

Great Granny Pillow

Assemble four Fabric D rectangles to the Great Granny Strip Unit by matching centers for placement.

Make one Great Granny Block Unit.

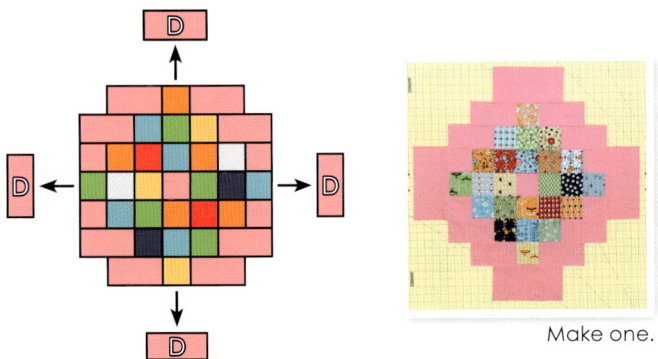

Make one.

Center a 20 ½" square ruler on the Great Granny Block Unit. I like to use the Creative Grids 20 ½" Square Ruler.

Trim Great Granny Block to measure 20 ½" x 20 ½".

Make one.

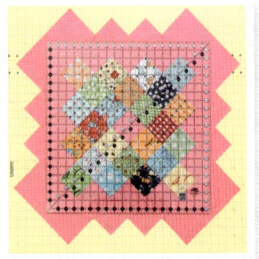 

Make one.

Borders:

Attach side borders using the Fabric E strips.

Attach top and bottom borders using the Fabric F strips.

Pillow Top should measure 24 ½" x 24 ½".

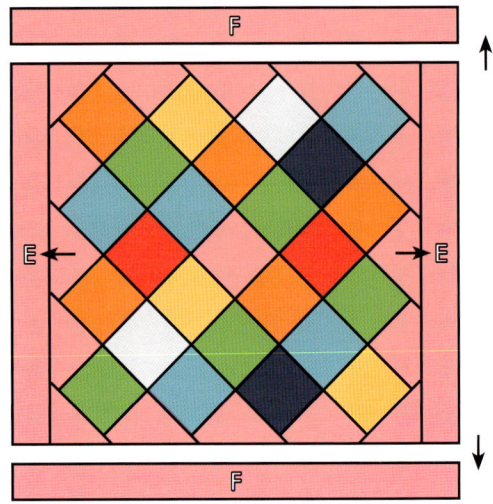

Pillow Top:

Layer the Pillow Top, the Batting and the Fabric I square.

Quilt Pillow Top as desired.

Baste ⅛" around the inside of the Pillow Top.

Trim excess batting and muslin.

Pillow Back:

With wrong sides facing, fold a Fabric G rectangle in half.

Folded Fabric G Unit should measure 16" x 28".

Make two.

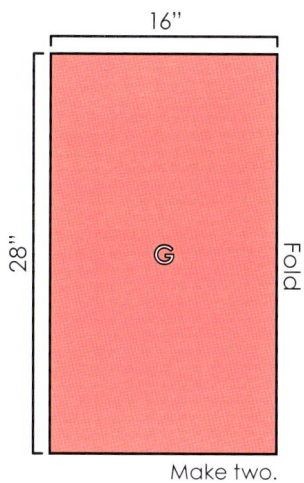
Make two.

Pillow Assembly:

Layer two Folded Fabric G Units and overlap them 4" with folds in the center and raw edges on the outside.

Pin in place.

Pillow Back should measure 28" x 28".

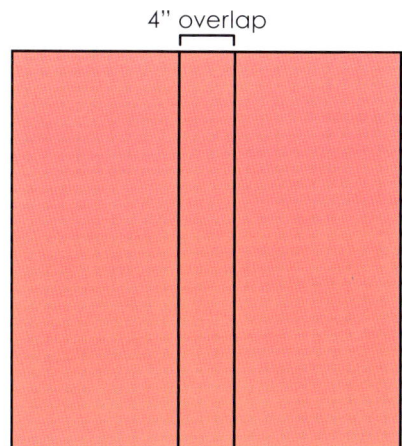

Mark the center of the Pillow Top and mark the center of the Pillow Back. Matching centers, layer the Pillow Top right side up on the Pillow Back.

Baste ⅛" around the edges to hold the Pillow Top and Pillow Back together.

Trim excess backing.

Finishing:

Piece 2 ½" Fabric H strips end to end for binding.

Bind as desired.

Great Granny Squared

34 Great Granny Squared

36 Great Granny Squared